Stranded on a Desert Island

A collection of poems to rescue and enlighten lost souls

Frank Navratil
Illustrations by Jana Navratilova

(written and illustrated during the Covid-19 pandemic)

Stranded on a Desert Island

© 2022 Frank Navratil
Illustrations © Jana Navratilova
All rights reserved

For Jana Navratilova
Thank you for rescuing me from my desert island

CONDITIONS OF SALE

This book is sold subject to the condition that it will not by any method be lent, re-sold, rented out or otherwise circulated without the publisher´s written consent in any form of binding or cover including electronic form, other than that in which it is published.

www.middlewaymindtraining.com

First Edition
Published by Frank Navratil
Purkynova 1246/9
Ricany, Czech Republic

ISBN **978-80-88022-19-0**

Contents

Stranded on a Desert Island 1
Uncertainty 3
Why am I still here? 6
Drifting 8
Bardo 9
Thoughts, Words and Deeds 11
Angel of the Night 13
The First Encounter 15
My Clinical Environment 18
My Unborn Child 20
Be Mindful of Me 22
Buddha Nature 25
I am a Wave 27
Drowning in your Blue-Green Oceans 28
I Feel Peace 29
The Warmth of the Heart 31
Immeasurable 33
Beginner's Mind 35
When I am Old 37
Hope 39
No Mind is an Island 40

Stranded on a Desert Island

This island that surrounds us
where many ships have landed
They try to lend a helping hand
but we stay lost and stranded

We chase each endless battle
causing pain along the way
The distance between all of us
grows further day by day

Possessed by our addictions
Our head stuck in the sand
We escape the painful truth
losing track of where we stand

We believe we really can
purchase every dream
Amassing greater wealth
while losing our esteem

We focus all our strength
We strive to be the best
Enriching our net worth
to be better than the rest

So much time is wasted
So much time is lost

We live as if forever
but we always pay the cost

We remember when we fall
or when our death is near
We only think of changing
when our life is faced with fear

We inflict harm to get ahead
What we sow is what we reap
No one may ever judge us
but the secret will never sleep

Behold the law of karma
and let destiny unfold
Can we learn this lesson
long before we get too old

Who will send that ship
to rescue all our souls
and take us back in time
so we can fill up all the holes

We wander through this life
climbing up and down each hill
but will we have the wisdom
to reach out if we´re still….
stranded on a desert island

Uncertainty

One can only wonder at the world sometimes,
for its sad misgivings, its mad upbringings
the never-ending unanswered seas of separation
transcending the entire universe
saturating and permeating our very humble souls

Anything more would spell a curse
for those who seek refreshment from a dry bottomless well

Mortal eyes genuflect to majestic mountain Gods
Inner strength reflections emanate from
dark emerald pools of consciousness
They flow endlessly like molten stone
The burdened fluid longing and yearning
to freely trickle though crevices of destiny

The truth unveils its nakedness under only scrutinous eyes
A magnifying glass can decipher but can also sear
beneath the baked glow of the summer sun.

Distant cries beckon,
Feeble handshakes of freedom slip away
into the oblivion of desertion
deep into the solitary confines of mortality
The arena of wisdom presides however

while the actors take the stage
Minute by minute
occurrence by occurrence
The sands of time weave the yarns of
reason and confusion
sin and salvation
satiation and deprivation
into mottled fabrics of contradiction

Beneath the shadow cast, lies a glimmer of light
Inclement weather subsides
Ships sail calmly over seas of forbidden darkness
Informers converge and consummate new ground
before death lays its whimsical hand of certainty upon all fearful

We send out the song whose melody seeks civilization
of the mind dance of happiness

We send out the memory that simply desires reason
of all that crumbles yet rises from the dead

We send out the bubble of hierarchic dominance
and let it float and reaffirm its integrity amongst the galaxies

We send out the dark angels of pathos that leave us
at the end of the world's rhetoric

We send out the prince whose insatiable conquests
transfer gold into fire and diamonds into dust

We send out the spirit who seeks out our chosen destiny
amongst life's infinite tributaries

We send out the holy shroud to cloak who we believe is the giver of life,
the warmth of the sun, the chosen one

Lastly, in a symphony of hope
We set free the birds, whose wings of flight
carry us safely beyond the reaches of our gains,
across the darkened misty plains of
uncertainty

Why am I still here?

At least a thousand lifetimes
building castles in the sand
barely treading water
grasping anything I can

Longing for the answers
to dissipate my fear
I should be in a better place
but why am I still here?

Moving one step forward
falling two steps back
filled with fame and fortune
but it's happiness I lack

I climb another mountain
I reach another tier
I should be feeling satisfied
but why am I still here?

I build walls around my island
judging everything outside
It all comes back to haunt me
There is no place left to hide

So much that I have wanted
The path was once so clear
I should have finally reached that place
but why am I still here?

I have hurt so many people
I have stepped on many friends
Just to fall the victim
on a path that never ends

I still have much to learn
The end is far from near
Another chance to make it right
That's why I am still here.

Drifting

distances along

miles of outstretched seas

experiences longing to be shared

the gap grows and bridges fade

the waves wash up

lost memories along the shore

waiting to appear on the surface

like a weathered piece

of driftwood or polished snow white shell

you ask yourself,

"where did that come from?"

drifting…….

then when you finally reach the end

you realize there´s just more distance,

more empty space

or just maybe

you have been running around

in circles

and back to where you started from

distance is dangerous

a silent displacement

a lonely disposition

a boat with no oars

just drifting….

Bardo

intermediate suspension
between
one dimension and
the next
a fracture between the
cracks
a pause between
breaths
the time before
a change
an interval
from one time
to the
future
the silent interlude
between
the first and
second notes
a recess between
act one and
act two
a change in direction
a thoughtless space
a mountain divide
the rest
between each
heartbeat

and the gap
between each
thought
of the past to
that of future
the rift
there
in the present moment
there
in the chasm of uncertainty
there
in that place
after I lose
and
before I gain
between what I know
and
what I seek to understand
I find
all I need
here in the void
I am at peace
here
I am alive
here I choose to reside
here
I am awake.

Thoughts, Words and Deeds

I come back here with regret
for what I was led to do
as it began with just one thought
that I could not quarantine

My mind was not aware
as that single moment passed
and little did I know
how little control I had

But now it's all too late
as I cannot take it back
I left an open door
for that virus to escape

The genesis of thought
from my infected mind
where ego grasps a hold
and emotions just run wild

There I may still diffuse
a bomb that will explode
but anger knows no bounds
and thoughts transform to words

Uttered in such a way
to inflict a world of pain
with rampant fits of rage
the predator attacks its prey

Obsessed with no control
forced to make the crime
deeds of unbridled passion
poisoned spaces of my mind

Losing all I know
empty oceans deep inside
becoming just that person
that I never thought I'd be

Now I plant my thoughts
being mindful of their ways
let them grow from loving hearts
to tender words and wholesome deeds.

Angel of the Night

I was once someone who mattered
I was once someone who cared
Now my book's full of empty pages
and they're scattered everywhere

Every moment passes by me
Every day, then every year
As I stare through my empty bottle
I'm too scared to even shed a tear

So please, take me back home again
My angel of the night
Take me back home again

Because the road I knew has faded
You're my only hope in sight
Take me home my angel of the night

Spend my whole day chasing handouts
so I can get myself some more
They think they're really trying to help me out
but they don't know why I'm out here for

It's the only thing that's left to love
Let me be the eternal slave

Cause the only time I have to think
is when I wake up from my grave

So please, take me back home again
My angel of the night
Take me back home again

If there was no one who ever loved me
Then you're my only hope in sight
Take me home my angel of the night

The First Encounter

Lost in the doldrums of predictable existence
Myriads of faceless crowds in the streets
Blank generic minds

From beneath the shadowed avenues
a form, a radiance approaching

She appears as a rainbow
Light against the soft stream
of perspiration from my brow

My heart is arrested by her delicate lines
Her neck slender as a swan

I watch in wonderment, transfixed
My mind loses weight and vision blurs
From the depths I surface

I try to move forward
A gallant horseman to her rescue
Swept from harm's way
My mind detonates the command
I progress in emotion but remain still as a stone statue

She draws air from my lungs,

consuming my breath

and cradles me from my lonesome descent

She move like piano keys along melodic scales

Her form traces the classical curve of the Stradivarius

Her silhouette paints a portrait against a moonlit sky

Her magnetic eyes invite

as the warmth of fire on a cold night

Her smile radiates

as the first break of sunshine on an otherwise clouded sky

To catch a glimpse transforms many,

the vagrant streetwalker stands tall

the rich and noble are humbled

the hardest hearts soften

She inspires hope for even the bitterest of souls

and provides direction in the deepest darkest forests

She embodies the innocence of a newborn

yet has the strength to render useless the wars of man

Her dance ignites peak thresholds of emotion

My mind races with refreshment

Raindrops against my face

I inhale her as she occupies my lungs
As I exhale she is carried swiftly by the wind
The first encounter retreats into vaults of memory
The illusion of perfection remains,
clothes that will never wear
colors that will never fade

For one moment in time,
I watched as the world stood still
and soared with the angels
to a carnival where the carousel never stops

I gather my things and begin my journey back into time,
as I blend like the changing seasons
back into the faceless crowd again

My Clinical Environment

A smoothly clinical environment is nice
a way I like to keep it
An uncluttered expanse like prairie land
seems really what fairs well

Outside, the insidious sirens bellow
the dirt, the filth, the sanitary engineer
invade a personal peaceful domain
and draw one's soul into kaleidoscopes of chaos
and into doubts that perpetually linger

But everything has a place inside, a predetermined spot
stamped and sealed by definite commitment
justified by its very existence, time and time again
never failing, nor ever faltering

No crayon-coloring outside the lines
No hesitation, no decision teetering on jagged mountain peaks
Only the smooth, sanded lines of an empty table
like an intestine cleansed by dietary fiber

The pelting rain splatters against the window
casting a grey gloom of reminder
Thunders of human screams in the darkness
The twisted pain snaking through shades of murderous intent

The slaves of compromise and acceptance grounded
like a sparrow with a broken wing

The deadbolt smiles a familiar face
and seals a lost fate,
while the mist of intoxicating silence pervades within
Within once again a clinical pacification
like a blind man's sudden recognition of his own trodden land
as he falls Into the outstretched arms of a comfortable easy chair
and into a deep dreamless slumber.

My Unborn Child

I wait in haste for my unborn child
like an painter for works of art
or a writer for those radiant words
that stem straight from the heart

Deep within my aching womb
I plant my soul desire
Nurtured there it waits to be
born to light the fire

We all hope to bear the fruit
from a child we hold inside
Sometimes those dreams may ripen,
just lie dormant or subside

But now a barren wasteland
with scanty fertile ground
No seed of life can grow there
No spirit can be found

Impregnated expectations
lose their hold now day by day
I walk blindly through the forest
Trying hard to find my way

I say this now, with one deep sigh
and hope the time will come
but as it is in the house of life
so much is left undone

I may not meet my unborn child
but grateful none the less
For the gifts that come along my way
I am forever blessed

Be Mindful of Me

Hello?
Why are you not here?
Be mindful of me
for I am your present,
Be very mindful of me
I am the only dimension
in which you truly dwell

Why can you not see me now?
I am alive and vibrant
I am awake and ready
I have the ability
to enable your life
and ignite the flame

Why are you still asleep?
At this very moment
I am available for you
with so much to offer
so much to share
but you choose to be absent

I am not your past
That place is a barren land
forever dead and abandoned

laden with faded memories and regrets
Wake up and dance with me
There is no life back there

I am also not your future
I do not reside in your dreams
I am not your empty wishes
nor your flimsy fantasies
not even your baseless fears or worries
I am the real thing, here and now

I am your breath
as your chest rises and falls
I am the wind
as it embraces your face
I am your happiness
I am in each and every peaceful moment

I am your tranquil oasis
I am the radiance of the sun
I warm your very being
I exist here and I exist now
I am not just a cloud of thought
in your savage mind

I am an empty canvas
just waiting to be painted

With just a stroke of your brush
you can paint your journey
your life, your masterpiece
Come draw your work of art with me

If not mindful of me
you will soon wilt and wither away
for I am the sound you fail to hear
the attention in every detail
the smell, the touch, the image
to which you turn a blind eye

It may be a shame
that in this very human life
you have chosen not to live
Open your eyes and see what I am
Be mindful of me, I am always here with you
Here now, where happiness resides

Buddha Nature

Buried deep beneath
layers of clouded mind
free from incessant chatter
a bright and radiant light

a still and wave-less ocean
boundless stretch of sky
unhindered mind so open
to enter every doorway

temple of tranquility
shelter from every storm
core of tender kindness
effortless fountain of love

stream of childlike innocence
unshackled from the prison
unmistaken sense of clarity
refreshment for the soul

like a lost and sunken treasure
concealing precious jewels
each one can share the riches
and satisfy the hunger

from where we all become
before the cravings of despair
as we wander through samsara
in search of peace of mind

a face seen for the first time
like a reflection in a mirror
something we always held
but never really perceived

this is our very nature
our ultimate inner master
the truest state of mind
lies dormant until awoken

stand bold just as a mountain
to search the ancient truth
extinguish all the senses
let answers rise and surface

little time there is to spare
to grasp this inner truth
and find the source of light
the key to eternal bliss

I am a Wave

Who am I?
I am a wave
I am not one form
but forever changing a
dynamic impermanent flow
I arise then quickly pass away
just one short lifetime as I crest
and peak then look down from
high above only to realize
who I am, I am not alone
I am no better nor any
worse, different yet
still the same only
connected to others
who exist just like me
one common element yet

angry currents flow beneath
and howling winds blow strong
above, churning and turning as we
each crash against each other and
when the wind subsides and quiet
stillness prevails again we blend
into one tranquil and peaceful
ocean, no more differences
no more peaks, no more
valleys only then do
 we know who we
really are We
are one

Drowning in your Blue-Green Oceans

I see your rolling waves; they come and sweep me to the shore

and I know my love for you will stay forever more

and as you rise and crest against your silver sand

I can surface from the depths and reach out for your hand

So cradle me and carry me away

to another time and to another place

where I can be drowning in your blue-green oceans… of your eyes

Drowning in your blue-green oceans

Your kind of love is one that enters with your sound

and your faces change with no logic to be found

and I know now what I've always had to do

Search from deep within and spend my time with you

Hopelessly drifting with everything you do

Emotions are lifting and I'm drowning into you

and I know now what I've always had to do

Search from deep within and spend my time with you

So cradle me and carry me away

To another time and to another place

Where I can be drowning in your blue-green oceans… of your eyes

Drowning in your blue-green oceans

I Feel Peace

I feel peace...
when my mind is all so clear
when no clouds are ever passing
when I release my grip on fear

I feel tranquil...
when anguish leaves me from the past
when no worries grasp the future
when my anger cannot last

I feel bliss...
when I do not crave a thing
when what I need is what I have
when I accept what life will bring

I feel balance...
when my plans are made to change
when there seems no rhyme nor reason
when I'm forced to rearrange

I feel still...
when I pause to listen to my heart
when I breathe joy in every moment
when the world appears to fall apart

I feel peace…

when it comes from deep inside of me

when its strength cannot be shaken

when I can just let my mind be free

The Warmth of the Heart

From out of the sun's rays
comes the warmth of the heart
It flutters like a petal from a flower
It touches only those who are fortunate to believe
and sometimes passes in the flash of a moment
Its strength protects those who are afraid of the night
and stretches to the ends of the oceans,
farther than the eye can see.

It gives confidence to reach to the highest heavens
and gives shelter to those who are lost
Its actions know no words, nor expect reward
Its gentle embrace smiles
like the simple pleasure of holding hands
while walking on a sunny summer day

From out of the cold winter night
comes the anger of the wind
It howls against the waves of the sea
Like uncertainty, it knows no one direction
It is unforgiving and brings cold to the heart

Rain falls,
like tears on the cheeks of a little child
It cleanses the soul and brings forth new life

The air is calm and the wind is now silent
Peace again for the mind after the turbulent storm

From out of the stillness
comes a soft slow wind that carries with it
a warm memory of a time long ago
of a fallen petal from a flower of the past
It is but a trace that lingers in the mist
yet it is strong and mighty and endures deep in my soul.

Immeasurable

I choose to dwell
in the divine abodes,
though my tragic human life
has taken many different roads

Across the timeless oceans
to majestic mountain peaks
stranded on an island
while my mind forever seeks

The armour of compassion
a power I strive to wear
for a world that often suffers
a common burden we must share

May all of us be happy
may our lives be safe and sound
and may we all be healthy
where only peaceful hearts abound

Loving acts of kindness
that radiate from the core
a warm expanding light
a raft that takes us to the shore

When fortune is kind to others
but fails to pass my way
I will grasp the wisdom
a source of joy to hold today.

I maintain a perfect balance
When I rise or when I fall
an evenness of mind
an impartial love I give to all

Metta, karuna, mudita, upekkha
sacred virtues I hold so dear
anchored pillars of wisdom
the unshakeable truth I hear

The worldly treasures I often crave
though seem to appear so pleasurable
can never match the infinite minds
their boundless riches, immeasurable

Beginner's Mind

I was once the maestro
rigid and unyielding
blinded by my expertise
oblivious of my fatal delusion
a restricted mind
traversing narrow alleys
only to encounter
barricades of resistance
my mask of brilliance confined
within closed doors of ignorance

Now, I cultivate a beginner's mind
an open inquisitive sky
without clouds of arrogance
a wisdom in uncertainty
breath of virgin air
I graciously accept
all that I will never know
always the apprentice
never the master
willing to learn
willing to step forward
the innocence of a child
a clear untainted vision
soft and malleable

full of wonder and excitement

free from opinions and views

free from misconceptions

no expectations no convictions

empty of any judgment

with an expansive mind

I am open

to infinite possibilities

like empty pages of a book

I wait to be written

I listen more deeply

I see more clearly

I understand so much more

my cup filled with curiosity

as I follow my intuition

detached from the grips of ego

my beginner's mind

stays forever present

and wide awake

to the full experience

that awaits me

When I am Old

When I am old.
what will I do?
When I am old
and my days left are few

Will I regret
the things I have done?
Will I sing to the sky
or pray to the sun?

When I am old
Will I be wise?
Will you see a true heart
when I look in your eyes?

When I am old,
will I dwell in the past?
Will I live in the moment
and make each day last?

When I am old
will I still understand?
Will I act with compassion?
Will I reach out my hand?

When I am old,
and I've done all I could
Did life give me meaning
that I hoped that it would?

Will each crease on my face
mark the time I felt pain?
or will each be a sign
I was once born again?

There is still some time
before I get old
to make those amends
at least I've been told

I must not waste a day
for life is a flower
and each day is a gift
only passing by the hour

Hope

the vice loosens
thoughts expand
a new world emerges
demons disband

a flash of a moment
a taste you can savour
perception transforms
and enlightens the flavour

a prospect of blue sky
a buoyant burst of love
from out of the clouds
appears the flight of a dove

No Mind is an Island

My agitated mind
consciousness in slumber
sleepwalking through life
forever grasping on to dreams
and clinging to eternal desires

Like a bird attempting to fly
but never leaving the ground
never really free from the shackles
of my delusions

Expecting, longing, craving…
for fleeting moments of passing joy
while suffering and watching hopelessly
as they arise and dissolve
into the entrenched reality of impermanence

There seems no end on the horizon
for its gripping hold spares no one
as it binds me to futile memories and insatiated wishes
blinding me from the present moment
that only time when I am living
and that only time of inner peace and awakening

No mind is an island

No wave in the ocean is alone

Not a precious breath can be stolen

Not a trace of I can be found

My tranquil mind

consciousness awoken

a limitless expanse of sky

never to dwell in the realms of the non-living

unlocked from the brutal hold

that my senses desire

Awareness and clarity in focus

free from ignorance and illusion

independent from the burden of fear

I can feel myself lifting

and rising above the clouded sky

the weight of a million lifetimes

released from my aching mind

All the outside now blends with the inside

my island has ceased to exist

as it spans across the horizon

it becomes one with the oceans,

one with the sky and reaching

to the endless expanse of eternity

No mind is an island

No wave in the ocean is alone

Not a precious breath can be stolen

Not a trace of I can be found

www.ingramcontent.com/pod-product-compliance
Lightning Source LLC
LaVergne TN
LVHW090040080526
838202LV00046B/3895